Welcome!

Welcome to a captivating journey into the realm of the bizarre and revolting! In these pages, you'll discover a treasure trove of peculiar tidbits and stomach-churning curiosities!

If you've ever wanted to explore the weird, wacky, and downright gross aspects of our world, this book is your passport to an unforgettable adventure through the extraordinary and the icky. Strap in, and let's dive headfirst into the strange and slimy underbelly of facts!

Table of Contents

STRANGE FACTS

GROSS FACTS

Strange: Abnormal Animals

1. Sea Cucumber Defense: Some species of sea cucumbers can shoot their internal organs out their anus to deter predators.

2. The Great Poop Escape: When an Australian water beetle is swallowed by a toad, it heads straight for the toad's rear end, making the toad poop it out, alive and well.

3. Hibernation in the Desert: The African lungfish can encase itself in a slimy mucus cocoon and hibernate for up to four years.

4. Playing Dead: Opossums will "play dead" when threatened, falling limp, and excreting a foul-smelling fluid.

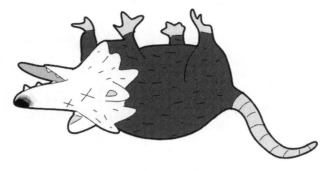

5. Eating Rocks: Crocodiles swallow large rocks, which sit in their stomachs. This helps them dive deeper and also helps their stomach grind up their food.

6. Cannibal Spiders: The female redback spider will sometimes eat the male after mating.

7. Narwhal's Mysterious Tusk: The long tusk of the narwhal is actually an inside-out tooth, that grows in a spiral. It's actually their only tooth!

8. Malachite Sunbird Nest: The male malachite sunbird seals the female inside her nest after mating, leaving only a small hole to feed her though. He does this to make sure that no other males can access her.

9. Dolphins' Sponging Technique: Some dolphins use marine sponges to protect their snouts while foraging on the seafloor.

10. Penguin Proposals: When penguins fall in love, they search the beach for the smoothest pebble and present it to their chosen penguin as a gift. If they take it, they're engaged!

11. Tough Birds: Woodpeckers slam their heads into wood around 20 times a second. But don't worry—they don't get headaches!

12. Panda Potty: Male pandas often do handstands to pee. They do this in order to leave their mark higher up on a tree.

STRANGE &
GROSS FACTS

Strange: Aliens & Outer Space

1. The Phoenix Lights: In 1997, thousands of people in Arizona, reported seeing large V-shaped formations of lights in the sky. The event remains one of the most significant mass UFO sightings in history.

2. E.T. Phoning Home: The famous line, "E.T. phone home" from the 1982 movie, became one of the most iconic phrases ever in film history.

3. Freaky Footprints: The Apollo astronauts' footprints on the moon will probably stay there for at least 100 million years.

4. UFO Day: World UFO Day is celebrated on July 2nd, commemorating the supposed UFO crash Roswell, New Mexico.

5. Alien Invasions: The 1938 radio drama "War of the Worlds," about an alien invasion, was so realistic that it caused a mass panic among listeners who believed it was an actual news broadcast.

6. Space Suit Flatulence: Space suits come with charcoal filters to handle, among other things, the astronauts'... farts.

7. Space Smells: Astronauts have described the smell of space as a combination of gunpowder, seared steak, raspberries, and rum.

8. Crop Circles: Mysterious patterns in crops, known as crop circles, have often been associated with UFO activity.

9. No Laundry in Space: The International Space Station doesn't have a washing machine. Instead of washing their dirty clothes, astronauts throw them away.

10. Far Out: If you could fly a plane to Pluto, the trip would take more than 800 years!

11. Galactic Alcohol: In space, there's a giant cloud that contains a billion-billion-billion liters of alcohol. Sadly, most of it is methanol, which is not the drinkable kind!

12. Space Diapers: When going on spacewalks, astronauts wear special diapers called MAGs made with a chemical that can absorb up to 1,000 times its weight!

STRANGE
& GROSS
FACTS

Strange: Unusual Sports Facts

1. Longest Tennis Match: The longest tennis match took 11 hours and 5 minutes to complete over three days at Wimbledon in 2010.

2. Golf Luck: The chances of making two holes-in-one in a round of golf are one in 67 million.

3. Get Your Steps In: On average, a soccer player runs about 7 miles during a single match.

4. Cheese Rolling: In England, there's an annual event where participants chase a 9lb wheel of cheese down a steep hill. The first person to cross the finish line wins the cheese.

5. No Lefties Allowed: In polo, players are forbidden to play left-handed, a rule established for safety reasons.

6. Stinky Hockey: Before rubber was invented, hockey pucks were made out of frozen cow dung!

7. Wrong Way Run: During the 1929 Rose Bowl, a player named Roy Riegels ran 65 yards in the wrong direction, resulting in his team losing the game.

8. Literally, A Basket: The very first game of basketball was played with a soccer ball, and instead of shooting it into a hoop, players aimed for a peach basket.

9. Up-Side-Down Sport: There is a sport known as "Headis," which is like table tennis, but players use their head to hit the ball, not paddles.

10. Running Backwards: There's a sport knows as "retro running" where participants run races backwards!

11. Bad Sportsmanship: In a Paraguay soccer match in 1993, the referee issued 20 red cards, sending off every player on both teams!

12. Fastest, Fruitiest Marathon: Patrick Wightman ran the 2012 London Marathon dressed as a banana in a time of 2 hours, 47 minutes, and 9 seconds.

STRANGE & GROSS FACTS

Strange: Funky Food Facts

1. Stinky Fruit: The durian fruit is banned in many public places in Southeast Asia because of its strong odor, which is often described as a mix of rotten onions and gym socks.

2. Delicious Ants: In some cultures, ants are considered a delicacy. They are often used in dishes like ant chutney and chocolate-covered ants.

3. Take Your Ketchup: Ketchup was originally used as a medicine in the 18th century and was believed to cure diarrhea and indigestion.

4. That's a Lot of Pizza: The world's largest pizza was made in 2012, measured 13,580.28 square feet (1,261.65 square meters). It took 11 hours to cook.

5. Pricey Spice: Saffron is one of the world's most expensive spices. One pound of saffron can cost upwards of $5,000!

6. Feelin' Hot, Hot, Hot: Chili Pepper X holds the record as the world's hottest chili pepper, with an average heat rating of over 2.69 million (jalapeño peppers are typically between 2,000-8,000 heat rating)!

7. Big Burger: The Guinness World Record for the largest hamburger weighed 2,014 pounds (914 kg)!

8. Historic Honey: Archaeologists have found pots of honey in ancient Egyptian tombs that are over 3,000 years old and still edible.

9. Cat Coffee: There is a type of coffee that is made from coffee beans that have been eaten and then pooped out by cats. The beans are collected from the feces, cleaned, and roasted to make coffee, which is considered a delicacy.

10. Creative Kit Kats: In Japan, they have a variety of flavored Kit Kat bars, including wasabi, sake, sweet potato, and green tea.

11. The Golden Roll: The world's most expensive sushi roll was sold for $1,978 in Japan. It was made with 5 premium ingredients, including caviar and gold leaf.

12. Pounds of Pasta: The world's largest bowl of spaghetti was created in California in 2010. It used 5,000 pounds of pasta and 2,000 pounds of sauce.

Strange: Spirits & Spells

1. Say Cheese: It was once believed that taking someone's photograph would steal their soul!

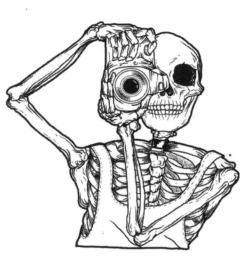

2. King Tut's Curse: King Tut's curse says that those who dared to open his tomb would suffer bad luck or death. The curse was created after several people associated with the tomb's discovery died under mysterious circumstances.

3. Shoe Magic: In some cultures, it's believed that hiding a shoe in the walls of a house can protect the people living there from evil spirits.

4. Poor Rabbit: Carrying a rabbit's foot is considered good luck for many people (but definitely not for the rabbit!).

5. Spilled Salt: Accidentally spilling salt is considered bad luck in many cultures, but throwing a pinch over your left shoulder is supposed to ward off any negative effects.

6. Broken Mirror: Breaking a mirror and getting seven years of bad luck is a common superstition. This may stem from the ancient Romans, who believed that life renewed itself every seven years.

7. Love Potions: Love spells and potions have been popular throughout history. Many recipes involved odd ingredients like a lover's hair or the wing of a bat.

8. Beware of Witches' Cheese: In Medieval Europe, it was believed that "witches' cheese" (a type of fungus) was used in concocting spells.

9. Binding Spells: In ancient Greece and Rome, people wrote curses on tablets and then bound or pierced them with nails to activate the curse. These are known as "curse tablets."

10. Broomstick Parking Only: The image of witches flying on broomsticks might come from rituals, where women "rode" brooms in fields to  "teach" the crops how high to grow.

11. Spell Ingredients: Traditional spell ingredients can be quite peculiar. Bat's blood, eye of newt, and toe of frog...many of these names are just colorful terms for common herbs. For example, "eye of newt" is often just mustard seed.

12. The Deadly Lake: Lake Natron in Tanzania turns animals into stone-like statues. Due to its high pH levels, animals that die in this lake get calcified, appearing as eerie statues.

STRANGE & GROSS FACTS

Strange: Silly & Strange Holidays

1. The Night of the Radishes: "The Night of the Radishes" takes place on December 23rd in Oaxaca, Mexico. People sell radishes that they've carved into nativity scenes and animals. The creator of the best radish carving wins a prize.

2. National Hug Your Cat Day: In the U.S., June 4th is celebrated as "National Hug Your Cat Day." People are encouraged to give their cats a deep squeeze to show them their love.

3. Punch Your Neighbor: The Tinku Festival is also known as "Punch Your Neighbor in the Face Day!" It is an old religious holiday celebrated every May in parts of Bolivia. People quite literally are encouraged to beat each other up. The more blood, the better the harvest!

4. Nose Picking Day: Studies show that up to 99% of people pick their noses. That is why a holiday was created to celebrate it! April 23rd is "National Nose Picking Day" – the one day of the year when it's acceptable to do some picking in public!

5. Christmas Eve in Norway: On December 24th, while many kids around the world are awaiting a visit from Santa Claus, some Norwegians are hiding their brooms. They believe witches roam the night sky on Christmas Eve, so they hide all their brooms so that the witches can't get to them.

6. Cockroach Racing Day: Cockroach racing is extremely popular in Australia, so they made a holiday to celebrate it! "Cockroach Racing Day" is every year on January 26th. The biggest event has 14 different types of races including a steeple chase!

7. Bean Throwing Day: Setsubun takes place in Japan on the day before the start of spring. It's part of ushering in spring and getting rid of bad spirits—and to do so, revelers pelt an elder member of their family with roasted soybeans.

8. Talk Like a Pirate Day: Ahoy Matey! One day out of every year, grab your eye patch and practice your "Argggs". "Talk Like a Pirate Day" is celebrated on September 19th.

9. Baby Jumping Festival: Every June, a small Spanish village celebrates the "Baby Jumping Festival". Villagers dress up like devils. Then, babies born during the previous year are laid on mattresses in the street while the costumed devils leap over them.

10. La Tomatina: On the last Wednesday of every August, around 30,000 people make their way to a small town in Spain to participate in the world's biggest food fight. It is a tomato-throwing frenzy, usually lasting for about an hour, and fire trucks are brought in afterwards to wash the streets.

11. Picnic Day: "Picnic Day" is a public holiday held in northern Australia on the first Monday of August. This is a day off for most businesses and schools, and it encourages locals and visitors to enjoy a picnic in nature, a park or on a beach.

12. Squirrel Appreciation Day: January 21 is "Squirrel Appreciation Day," a day to acknowledge the role that squirrels play in nature and how cute their fluffy tails are.

Strange: Medical Mysteries

1. Spontaneous Human Combustion: Throughout history, there have been accounts of people mysteriously catching fire without any apparent external source of ignition.

2. The Dancing Plague: In 1518, a woman began dancing in the street, and within a week, hundreds were dancing. Many died from heart attacks, strokes, or exhaustion. The exact cause remains unknown.

3. The Sleeping Sickness:
Between 1917 and 1928, a half million people were affected by encephalitis lethargica, which left them in

statue-like states, speechless and motionless. The cause remains a mystery.

4. Cotard's Syndrome: A rare mental disorder in which people believe they're dead, missing organs, or don't exist at all.

5. Morgellons Disease: Patients feel as if parasites are crawling underneath their skin and often report strands coming out of their pores.

6. The Sweating Sickness: In the 1500s, England was struck by a mysterious sickness that caused severe sweating, pain, and fatigue, often leading to death within hours. The illness disappeared, and its cause remains unknown.

7. Mary Mallon ("Typhoid Mary"): Mary was an asymptomatic carrier of typhoid fever. She infected numerous people in the early 1900s while showing no symptoms herself.

8. Hearing Voices: Some people who are deaf report hearing voices, a phenomenon that challenges our understanding of auditory hallucinations.

9. Déjà Vu: That eerie feeling that you've experienced something before, even if it's entirely new, is common but not well-understood from a neurological standpoint.

10. The Placebo Effect: Many patients experience real relief from symptoms when they take a sugar pill instead of real treatment. The power of belief in medicine is profound but not entirely understood.

11. Alien Hand Syndrome: A condition where a person's hand appears to take on a mind of its own, acting independently from the person's intentions.

12. Alice in Wonderland Syndrome: A condition where you see your body as giant or very tiny. Often seen in people with seizures.

STRANGE &
GROSS FACTS

Strange: Far-Out Fashion & Beauty

1. Zipper Accidents: Zippers have caused more injury than sharks. Be careful when you zip up!

2. Ancient High Heels: The first high heels were worn by Persian horse riders in the 10th century. They used the heels to help secure their feet in the stirrups.

3. Island Fashion: The Hawaiian Aloha shirt was originally made from leftover kimono fabric.

4. Hat Tax: England once had a tax on hats. If you had a hat, you were taxed, and if you were caught wearing one without a tax stamp, there was a hefty fine.

5. Not So White: The original color of the wedding dress wasn't white. Blue was the color of choice for brides in medieval Europe because it represented purity.

6. Buttons for Show: When buttons were invented, they were so expensive and trendy that people used to sew them onto their clothes just for decoration!

7. Denim's Humble Beginnings: Denim jeans were first worn by miners because of their durability, not by fashion influencers or cowboys.

8. King's Beard Tax: Peter the Great, put a tax on beards in 1705. He hoped it would encourage Russian men to adopt a clean-shaven look.

9. Nine Yards: The saying "to go the whole nine yards" came from WWII fighter pilots in the South Pacific. Gunners were armed with an ammunition belt which was 27 feet long. To use the whole belt was to go "the whole nine yards."

10. The Real Use of Pockets: In the 17th century, women's dresses had pockets large enough to fit a whole chicken.

11. Purple Royalty: In ancient Rome, only the emperors were allowed to wear purple clothing. It was the color of royalty and was made from a rare sea snail.

12. Crunchy Clothes: Silk is made from the fibers produced by silkworms when they form their cocoons. So, if you're wearing a silk shirt, you're essentially wrapped up in worm spit!

Strange: Unusual Records & Achievements

1. Longest Fingernails: In 2022, Diana Armstrong broke the record for the longest fingernails ever. Measuring 1,306.58 cm (42 ft 10.4 in), the combined length of Diana's fingernails is longer than a school bus!

2. Most Bees on a Person: In 2015, a beekeeper in China set a new world record after covering his body with almost 1.1 million bees!

3. Longest Hiccup Attack: The world record for the longest hiccup attack is held by Charles Osborne. He hiccuped for 68 years, from 1922 to 1990!

4. Heaviest Train Pulled with a Beard: In 2001 a man named Ismael Rivas Falcon pulled a train full of passengers (weighing 6,069 pounds / 2,753 kg) a distance of 32.8 feet or 10 meters just with the hairs of his chinny chin chin!

5. Spinning a Basketball on a Toothbrush the Longest: The longest duration spinning a basketball on a toothbrush is 1 min 47.4 sec, and was achieved by Ali Behboodifar, in Iran, in 2022.

6. Most Metal Eaten: Michel Lotito ate 9 tons of metal over the course of his lifetime, including a whole Cessna 150 airplane! Lotito suffered from Pica, which made him crave eating non-food objects like metal.

7. Most Feet and Armpits Sniffed: Madeline Albrecht was employed at a testing lab for products by Dr. Scholl. She worked there for 15 years and had to smell literally thousands of feet and armpits during her career. She has sniffed approximately 5,600 feet and thousands of armpits.

8. Most Pierced Woman: Elaine Davidson, a Brazilian-Scottish former nurse, is currently certified as the "Most Pierced Woman". It is reported that she currently has 4,225 body piercings. In a 2023 interview, she said her goal is to reach 20,000 piercings.

9. World's Tallest Dog: The world's tallest dog was Zeus, a Great Dane from Michigan. According to the Guinness Book of World Records, Zeus was 7 feet, 4 inches on his hind legs.

10. Most Big Macs Eaten: Donald A. Gorske is known as the "ultimate Big Mac fan," having eaten over 32,672 Big Macs in his lifetime.

11. The Most Steps Walked by a Dog Balancing a Glass of Water: The most steps walked by a dog while balancing a glass of water is 10, achieved by Sweet Pea, an Australian Shepherd/Border Collie, in 2008.

12. Longest Ear Hair: India's Anthony Victor has hair sprouting from the center of his ears that measures 7.12 inches (18.1 centimeters). The record was set in 2007 and remains to this day.

13. Big Burp: The longest burp on record is 1 minute 14 seconds and was achieved by Michele Forgione, at the 13th annual Hard Rock Beer festival, in 2009.

STRANGE & GROSS FACTS

Strange: Folklore & Fairy Tales

1. Hans My Hedgehog: The Brothers Grimm wrote a fairytale called, "Hans My Hedgehog." The fairytale is about a woman who gives birth to a human/hedgehog hybrid, who plays the bagpipes and rides around on a chicken.

2. Yeti Attack: Climbers of the Himalayan Mountain range are often warned about running into a yeti—a huge ape-like creature that wanders deep in the mountains. The creature walks on two legs, is covered in white hair, and is several times larger than a human.

45

3. Fairy Rings: Circular patterns of mushrooms are known as "fairy rings" because it was believed that they were caused by fairies dancing in a circle.

4. What an Ending: The French version of Rapunzel doesn't have a happy ending. Instead of finding a happily ever after, Rapunzel turns into a frog and the prince gets cursed with a pig's snout!

5. Leprechaun Sighting: In 1989, a local business-man in Ireland, claimed to have found evidence of a real leprechaun. After hearing a scream, he found bones, a tiny suit, and gold coins. The evidence is now displayed behind a glass case for visitors to come see.

6. Electric Avenue: Trolls are native to Norway and Sweden. Legend has it that the countries use electric fences to keep the trolls in their marked territory.

7. Bad Luck: Mermaids are often thought of as a beautiful, kind species, however this has not always been the case. As far back as 2,000 years ago mermaids were said to have meant bad luck and would lure sailors to their deaths.

8. Real or Myth: Did you know that there's been more than 1,000 official sightings of the Loch Ness Monster? A man named Gary Campbell runs the Official Loch Ness Monster Sightings Register. He started it after he spotted Nessie and had nowhere to report it.

9. A Grouchy Grandma: In one of the earliest tellings of Goldilocks and the Three Bears, Goldilocks isn't a cute little girl. Instead, she's a foul-mouthed old woman!

10. National Animals: The unicorn is the national animal of Scotland and feature in the Scottish Royal Coat of Arms. The red dragon is the national animal of Wales.

11. Green Children: A strange English legend called, The Green Children of Woolpit, tells the story of two green-skinned kids who mysteriously show up in the village of Woolpit. They would only eat green beans. Eventually they began eating other foods and their skin returned to normal color. It is still uncertain if this story is fact or fiction.

12. Disney Folklore: Many of Disney's most famous films are based on fairy tales like Cinderella, Snow White, Rapunzel, Pinocchio and more. In the movie Frozen, the plot is loosely based on the tale of The Snow Queen by Hans Christian Andersen. And in Frozen 2, the Nokk and other spirits have a basis in real folklore.

Gross: Earwax &
Other Gooey Things

1. Earwax Genetics: The type
of earwax you have (wet or dry)
is determined by your genetics.
People of East Asian descent
tend to have dry, flaky earwax,
while those of African or
European descent usually have
wetter, stickier earwax.

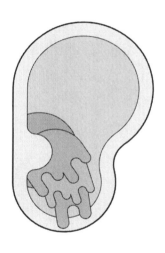

2. Self-Cleaning: Your ears are self-cleaning! Earwax
helps trap dust and other small particles, preventing
them from reaching the eardrum.

3. Bitter Taste: Some people, when they taste their
earwax (not recommended!), find it to be very bitter.

4. Mucus (Snot): Your body produces between 1 to 1.5 liters of mucus per day, even when you're healthy!

5. Vomit: Did you know that the stomach acid in vomit can erode tooth enamel? So, if you throw up, it's essential to wait an hour before brushing your teeth to avoid further damage.

6. Odor Origin: When you sweat, the bacteria on your skin break down the fats in sebum, which can produce an odor. Stress sweat smells worse than exercise sweat.

7. Infection Indicator: Pus is a thick yellowish or greenish liquid produced at sites of infection. It contains dead white blood cells, tissue debris, and bacteria.

8. Digestive Duties: Saliva contains enzymes that start the digestive process, breaking down some of the starches and fats in your food even before they reach the stomach.

9. Bile: Produced by liver and stored in the gallbladder, bile is a yellow-green fluid that aids in the digestion of fats. It's the bile that gives poop its typical brown color.

10. Hagfish Slime: When threatened, hagfishes can release a protein that, when combined with water, expands into a gelatinous and slimy substance. It can produce liters of this slime in mere minutes, which can choke and deter predators.

11. Whales: Blue whales have earwax plugs that can be several inches long! These plugs can offer a record of the whale's life.

12. Cats: Cats naturally produce less earwax than dogs. However, an excessive amount of dark wax (which resembles coffee grounds) can be a sign of ear mites.

STRANGE &
GROSS FACTS

Gross: What's That Smell?

1. Rotten Eggs: Caused by hydrogen sulfide, this scent is often associated with decaying organic matter and is notoriously foul.

2. Old Perfume: The world's oldest perfumes are over 4,000 years old! When archaeologists opened the bottles, they discovered scents reminiscent of pine, coriander, almond, and parsley.

3. Smelly Sweat: You can actually detect fear or disgust in human sweat, meaning emotions can have a very tangible smell!

4. Rain Aroma: You know that pleasant smell that often accompanies the first rain after a long period of warm, dry weather? It's called "petrichor." It arises from a mix of plant oils and chemical compounds.

5. Skunk Stink: A skunk's spray contains thiols, which are responsible for that notoriously foul odor. Tomato juice is a popular remedy for neutralizing skunk smell.

6. Vulture Vomit: Vultures have a particularly disgusting defense mechanism. When threatened, they will vomit up their latest meal as a deterrent. The smell is nauseating.

7. Corpse Flower: The titan arum, or "corpse flower," is a plant that, when in bloom, emits an odor reminiscent of a decaying mammal.

8. Feet Cheese: Limburger cheese is known for its strong smell, which is similar to foot odor. This isn't a coincidence – the bacterium used to ferment Limburger cheese is the same one responsible for human foot odor!

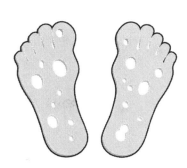

9. Rotting Shark: The smell of rotting shark carcasses is so repulsive to sharks that the U.S. Navy developed a "shark repellent" that mimicked this smell.

10. Swedish Herring: Surstromming is a Swedish delicacy made from fermented herring. Its smell is so overpowering that it is often eaten outdoors.

11. Ginko Tree Fruit: While the tree itself is lovely, the ripe fruit has a smell often compared to rancid butter or dog feces.

12. Freshly Cut Grass: Fresh cut grass has been shown to invoke feelings of summer and bring up outdoor memories for many people when they smell it.

Gross: Head Lice & Parasites

1. Fast Movers: Lice can move at a speed of up to 23 centimeters per minute.

2. Tongue Lice: The tongue-eating louse, enters a fish's gills, eats the fish's tongue, and eventually re-places the tongue by attaching its own body to the muscles that once held the tongue.

3. Specialized Claws: Head lice have six legs with claws at the ends, designed to grasp onto human hair.

4. Blood Buffet: Lice feed on human blood several times a day. When they bite, they inject their saliva which can cause itching.

5. Lice Lifespan: The lifespan of a head louse on a human host is about 30-days. Female lice can lay up to 10 eggs or "nits" a day.

6. Temperature Sensors: Lice have a built-in water and temperature sensor. They tend to move away from the base of the hair when they sense heat from a hair dryer or water during a shower.

7. Tapeworm Tidbits: Some tapeworms can grow up to 30 feet long inside the intestines of their host.

8. Flea Feasts: Fleas can consume blood over 15 times their body weight in a single day.

9. Mango Fly Maggots: These flies lay their eggs on

damp clothing or bed linens. When humans wear the infested clothing, the larvae penetrate the skin and develop into maggots inside the body, causing painful boils.

10. Bedbugs: Bedbugs inject an anesthetic when they bite, so the host (that's you!) doesn't feel it.

11. Blister Worm: The Guinea worm parasite enters the human body through contaminated drinking water. As it matures, it can grow up to 3 feet long. When it's ready to exit the body, it creates a painful blister, often in the legs or feet, and slowly emerges over the course of several days or weeks.

12. Eye Worm: The Loa Loa worm can migrate to the eye. Infected individuals can sometimes feel the worm crawling across their eye, and it can even be seen moving under the surface.

STRANGE &
GROSS FACTS

Gross: Sewers & Toilets

1. Fatbergs: Modern sewer systems often encounter 'fatbergs', which are large masses of congealed fat, wet wipes, and other waste that can block sewer pipes.

2. Sewer Tourism: Believe it or not, some cities offer sewer tours! For instance, in Paris, you can tour part of the city's sewer system and learn about its history.

3. Sewer Gators: 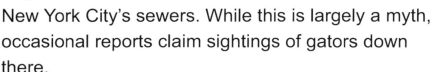 There's an urban legend that alligators live in New York City's sewers. While this is largely a myth, occasional reports claim sightings of gators down there.

4. Sewer Lights: Before electric lighting, some cities, like Birmingham, England, used sewer gases to power streetlights…must have been some smell!

5. River Dump: Before London's massive sewer network was constructed, the city's waste was dumped directly into the River Thames, leading to severe outbreaks of diseases like cholera.

6. Waste to Wealth: Sewers can contain valuable metals. A study in the U.S. estimated that the waste from one million Americans could contain as much as $13 million worth of metals, including gold and silver.

7. Toilet Names: A toilet or bathroom around the world goes by different names, including potty, privy, water closet, latrine, dunny, john, can, facility, restroom, washroom, powder room, lavatory, outhouse, convenience, bog, khazi, garderobe, cloakroom, throne room and many more.

8. Phone Flush: More than 7 million Americans have confessed to dropping their phones in the toilet.

9. Potty Pain: England's King George II died in 1760 after falling off his toilet.

10. Toilet Time: The average person uses about 57 sheets of toilet paper every day, and spends an average of 3 years of their life on the toilet.

11. Potty Party: In South Korea, there is an entire theme park and museum dedicated toilets. The main building is even shaped like a toilet seat!

STRANGE
& GROSS
FACTS

Gross: The Grossest Jobs on the Planet

1. Sewer Inspector: These workers delve into the underground world of sewage, often encountering waste, rodents, and various unspeakable items.

2. Proctologist: Specializing in the rectum, anus, and colon, these medical doctors treat a range of conditions that many might find off-putting.

3. Porta-Potty Toilet Cleaner: Cleaning and maintaining portable toilets, especially after large events, can be a very messy task.

4. Forensic Entomologist: They study insects on decomposing bodies to help determine the time of death.

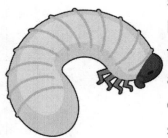

5. Maggot Farmer: Maggots are bred for various reasons, including fishing bait and medical applications, but the process of cultivating them can be rather stomach-turning.

6. Manure Inspector: Analyzing the quality and content of animal waste is essential for farming and fertilization but is undoubtedly a dirty job.

7. Gastroenterologist: This type of doctor examines the human digestive tract, which often involves procedures like colonoscopies.

8. Roadkill Collector: Someone must clean up animals that meet untimely ends on roads, and this job can be both sad and gross.

9. Odor Tester: Whether it's testing the efficacy of deodorants on actual armpits or checking the smell of breath fresheners, these testers must smell the good, the bad, and the very ugly.

10. Hazmat Diver: These divers plunge into polluted or toxic waters, often sewers or industrial sites, to perform necessary tasks or inspections.

11. Pest Controller: Dealing with infestations, whether it's roaches, rats, or other unwelcome guests, can be a challenging and gruesome task.

12. Landfill Operator: Managing the mountains of waste that societies produce is an essential job, but it involves being around garbage, decomposition, and associated smells daily.

STRANGE &
GROSS FACTS

Gross: Grossest Words

1. Phlegm: The term for the mucus we cough up can be unappealing.

2. Curdle: The process by which aging milk turns into curds.

3. Gurgle: The sound of liquid being agitated.

4. Ooze: The slow flow of a viscous fluid.

5. Fester: Referring to a wound that becomes septic.

6. Glob: A lump of a semi-liquid substance.

7. Sludge: A muddy or slushy mass.

8. Mucus: A slippery and sticky secretion that protects the mucus membranes in the body.

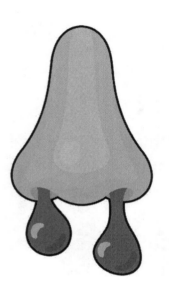

9. Rancid: Referring to fats or oils that have decomposed, often giving off an unpleasant odor.

10. Putrid: Decaying or rotting and emitting a fetid smell.

11. Bile: A bitter greenish-brown fluid that aids digestion and is secreted by the liver.

12. Pus: Pus is the yucky yellowish stuff that oozes out of an infected cut or pimple.

13. Queasy: The word queasy describes the feeling of nausea or wanting to vomit.

14. Scab: A scab is a hard, dry covering that forms over the surface of a wound. It is often crusty and itchy.

15. Feces: A.K.A. poop!

STRANGE & GROSS FACTS

Gross: Ancient Yucks!

1. Mummy Medicine: In medieval Europe, ground-up mummies were sold as medicine!

2. Gladiator Sweat: Ancient Romans believed that the sweat and blood of a gladiator could heal their ailments and even work as a cosmetic.

3. Urine Mouthwash: The ancient Romans also used human urine as a mouthwash and teeth whitener. The ammonia in urine was seen as an effective cleanser.

4. Honey Corpses: In ancient times, some cultures practiced "honey burial," where the deceased would be submerged in honey.

5. Loo Laundry: In ancient Rome, fermented urine was a key ingredient in the laundering process. The ammonia acted as a bleaching agent. The urine was often collected from public urinals.

6. Tooth Worms: Ancient cultures believed that cavities and toothaches were caused by "tooth worms." Some ancient dental treatments involved trying to coax the worm out or kill it.

7. Animal Dung Remedies: In ancient Egypt, remedies for various ailments often included animal dung. Crocodile poop, for example, was used as a treatment for wounds and infections.

8. Groom of the Stool: In Tudor England, the "Groom of the Stool" was a high-ranking position, serving as the restroom assistant to the king. The Groom was responsible for cleaning the king after he went potty.

9. Leech Therapy: For centuries, in both ancient Egypt and medieval Europe, leeches were used to drain one's blood as a way to cure various ailments.

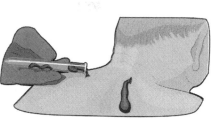

10. Roman Vomitorium: Certain rooms in the Roman feast halls were allegedly used by aristocrats to vomit so they could make space to eat more.

11. Tapeworm Diet: In the 19th and early 20th centuries, some people swallowed tapeworms to lose weight, letting the parasite consume the food inside their intestines.

12. Mouse Fur Eyebrows: In the Roman Empire, women who lost their eyebrows, or wanted thicker ones, would sometimes glue mouse fur in place of real eyebrows.

STRANGE & GROSS FACTS

Gross: Creepy, Crawly, Slimy, Slithery

1. Earwax-Eating Moths: Some species of moths, like the wax moth, have evolved to feed on earwax. They are attracted to the scent of earwax and can infest hearing aids if not cleaned regularly.

2. Mites and Eyelashes: Tiny mites called Demodex live in the hair follicles of humans and particularly in the eyelashes. They feed on dead skin cells and oil, and their presence can lead to skin and eye problems in some cases.

3. Carrion Beetle Parenting: Carrion beetles lay their eggs on dead animals. When the eggs hatch, the larvae feed on the decaying flesh, and the parents often join in on the meal.

4. Medicinal Maggots: Medicinal maggots are used in a medical practice known as MDT. Maggots are placed on wounds to help clean and heal them by consuming dead tissue.

5. Cockroach Resilience: Cockroaches are known for their resilience. They can survive in harsh conditions, including exposure to radiation. Some species of cockroaches can even live for up to a month without a head!

6. Snail Mucin Skincare: Snail mucin is harvested from snails (and it is believed to have various skincare benefits. It's commonly used in serums, creams, and masks.

7. Bullet Ants: The bullet ant, found in South America, has the most painful sting of any insect. The pain can last for hours and is likened to being shot.

8. Zombie Wasp: The jewel wasp will sting the cockroach in a specific area of its brain that controls the roach's escape reflex. Then it can control its brain— basically turning the cockroach into a zombie.

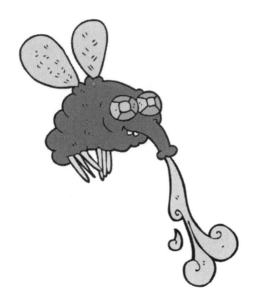

9. Fly Barf: Flies have a liquid diet, which means everything goes right through their digestive systems so nearly every time a housefly lands, it defecates or regurgitates. And for every human, there are 17 million flies, so that's a lot of barf!

10. Skin for Lunch: Dust mites are tiny spider-like animals that live everywhere we do. They eat dead skin cells and dander. .

11. Giant Earthworms: Some earthworm species can grow quite large. The Giant Gippsland Earthworm, can reach lengths of up to 3 feet (about 1 meter).

12. Liquid Lunch: A tarantula will inject its prey with venom, paralyzing it, then the enzymes within it will break down the body, turning it into a liquid.

13. Exploding Ants: Some ants make themselves explode when they're attacked. These ants split their skin open and coat their enemies in a yellow goo that either kills the intruder or hinders its attack.

Gross: Peculiar Potty Habits

1. Pee in Space: Astronauts aboard the International Space Station have a closed-loop system that recycles urine and converts it into drinking water.

2. Glowing in the Dark: Some species of fireflies use their poop to communicate. They produce bio-luminescent chemicals in their abdomens, which they release as "glowing poop" to attract mates.

3. Poo-Powered Cars: Researchers have developed bio-fuel made from human sewage. In 2010, a Volkswagen Beetle successfully completed a journey across the UK powered by this bio-gas.

4. Reindeer Pee Magic: There's a phenomenon known as "reindeer pee" that can make snow appear pink. This occurs when reindeer eat moss with a reddish pigment which turns the snow pink.

5. Ancient Pregnancy Tests: In ancient Egypt, women would urinate on barley and wheat seeds. If the barley sprouted, it was believed to be a sign of pregnancy. If the wheat sprouted, it indicated a baby boy.

6. Stinkiest Pee: Asparagus can make your urine smell really unusual. The compound responsible, mercaptan, is also found in skunk spray.

7. The "Perfect" Poop: There's actually a scale called the Bristol Stool Scale that categorizes poop into seven types, ranging from "hard lumps" to "liquid."

8. Poop Collectors: Some people collect coprolites, which are fossilized poop. These ancient fossils provide insights into the diets of prehistoric creatures.

9. Penguin Poop Bombs: Though Humboldt penguins are pretty small, scientists discovered that the birds can generate enough poo-propelling energy to send "poop bombs" flying at speeds of nearly 5 mph (8 km/h)!

10. Hippopotamus Projectile Pee: Hippos are known for their powerful urine streams. They can spray their urine up to 15 feet in the air as a territorial display.

11. Poo Paint: Male giraffes use their feces to mark their territory. They flick their tails while defecating, creating a scattering pattern known as "dung showers" on plants.

STRANGE & GROSS FACTS

Gross: Grossest Fair Foods

1. Ketchup Ice Cream: The Canadian National Exhibition in Toronto has a whole booth dedicated to ketchup and mustard flavored ice cream. Taste testers have said the ketchup flavor tastes like sour, rotten milk. Would you try it?

2. Python Kebabs: In Sacramento, California, you can fill your belly with python kebabs. The snakes are seasoned and grilled with peppers and onions. People say it tastes like chicken! Would you try it?

3. Buggy Apple: At the Wisconsin state fair you can buy a white chocolate and bug covered candy apple. The apple is dipped in white chocolate and then covered with edible June bugs, crickets, worms and ants. Some bugs are still crawling when you bite in! Would you try it?

4. Pickle Lemonade: If you're feeling thirsty at the South Florida Fair, you can indulge in some refreshing pickle lemonade. Would you try it?

5. Fried Butter Balls: If you love butter, at most fairs around the US you can try a big wad of deep-fried butter. It's definitely not good for you, but many people say it's actually delicious. Would you try it?

6. Donut Burger: At most county fairs you can get a delicious cheeseburger with donuts swapped out for the buns. The donut burgers are a sweet and salty delight—some even use jelly donuts! Would you try it?

7. Fried Jello: At the Utah state fair, you can often find fried Jello sticks. Locals say it's delicious! Would you try it?

8. Maggot Melt: If you're feeling adventurous, the California State Fair offers a Maggot Melt Sandwich. It's a grilled cheese sandwich with a heaping helping of maggots inside. Would you try it?

9. Chocolate-Covered Bacon: Fairs across the U.S. are known to sell chocolate-covered bacon. The bacon is cooked then dipped in chocolate and left to dry. Would you try it?

10. Deep-Fried Soda: Another favorite fair dessert is Fried Coke. Deep Fried Soda is a frozen cola-flavored batter that is deep-fried and then topped with Coca-Cola syrup, whipped cream, cinnamon sugar, and a cherry. Would you try it?

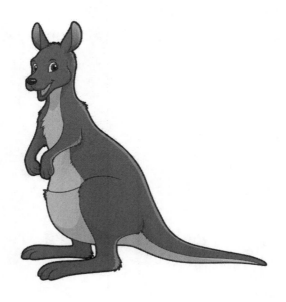

11. Kangaroo Delight: At the New York state fair, you can find kangaroo on a stick and kangaroo burgers. Kangaroo meat is said to taste like a mix between beef and lamb. Would you try it?

12. Cotton Candy Ice Cream Burrito: If you have a real sugar tooth you might want to try a Cotton Candy Ice Cream Burrito. A cloud of cotton candy is filled with three scoops of ice cream and rainbow sprinkles. Then it's rolled into a burrito and served as one colorful sugar rush. Would you try it?

STRANGE & GROSS FACTS

all DONE!

Congratulations! You now know a ton of strange and gross facts!

If you loved this Book, then you will love the rest of the Quiz Boss series of books, like:

 The Complete Book of FUN Riddles

 Would You Rather and More! - Boys Edition

 Would You Rather and More! - Girls Edition

 Would You Rather and More! - It's Summer Y'all

Find all our **Quiz Boss** books on Amazon, and don't forget to leave an honest review!

Made in United States
Orlando, FL
27 November 2023